Daisiejoy

Coloring Publishing Platform
First printing, 2019.

www.daisiejoy.com

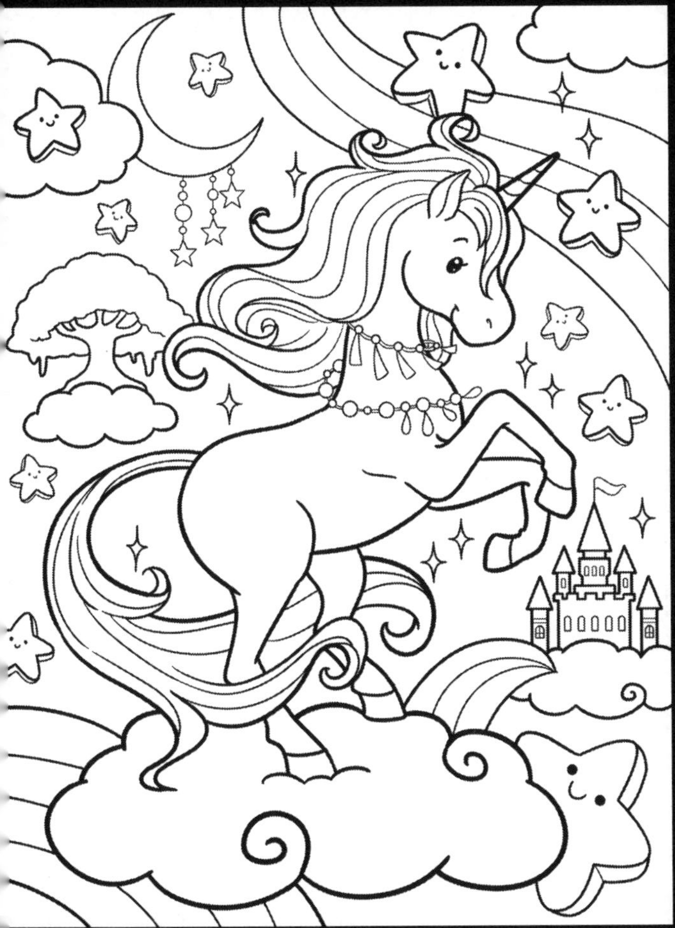

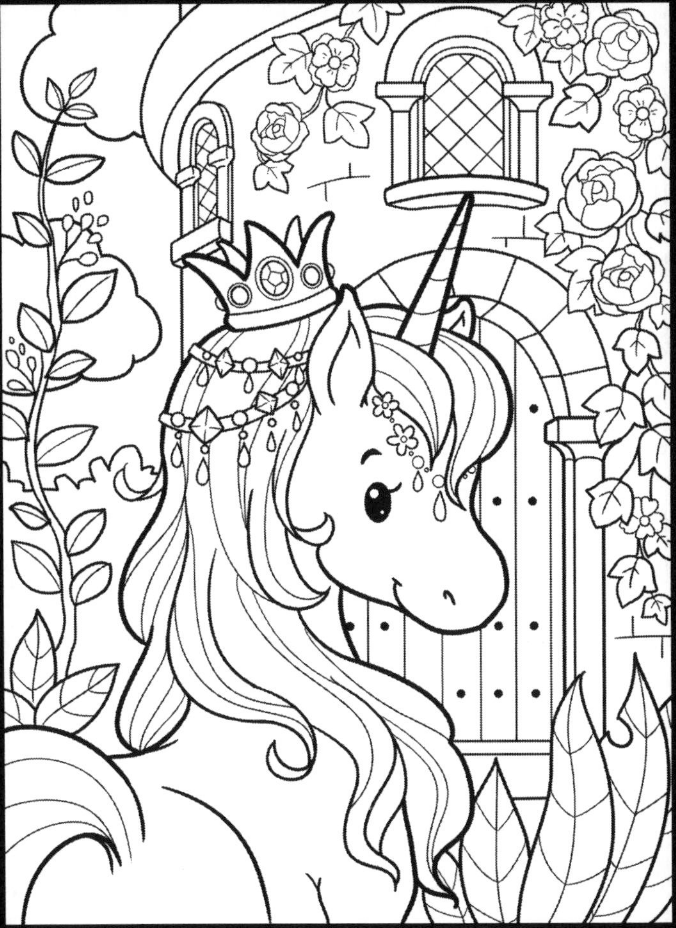

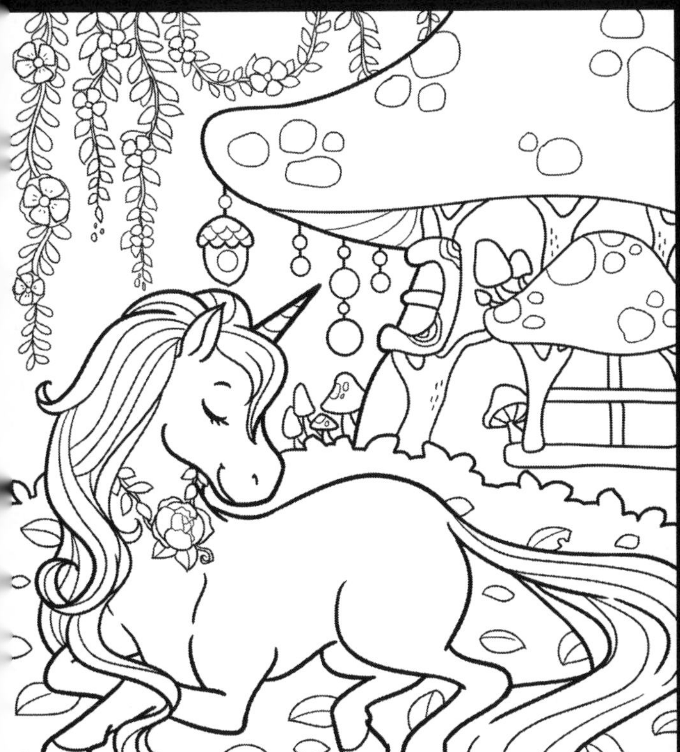

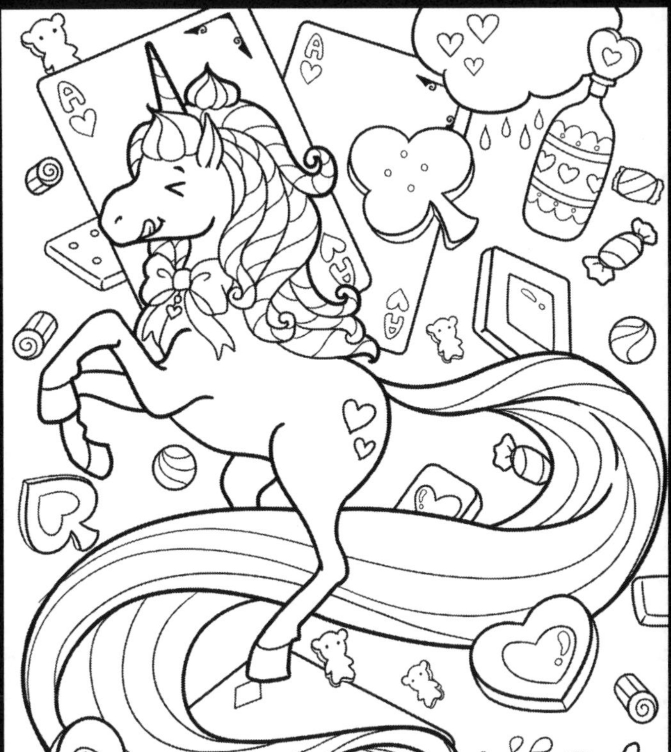

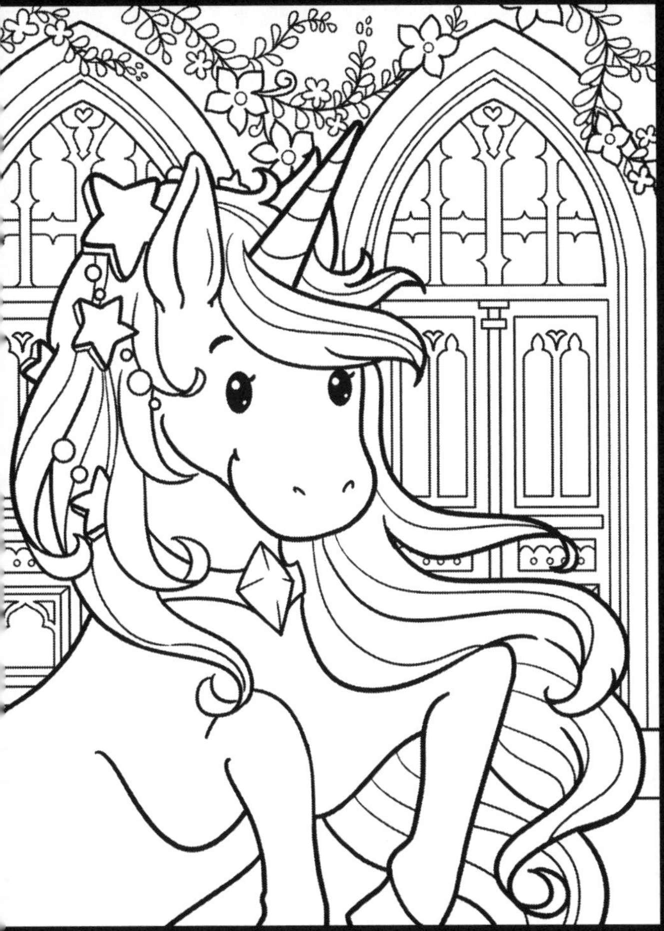

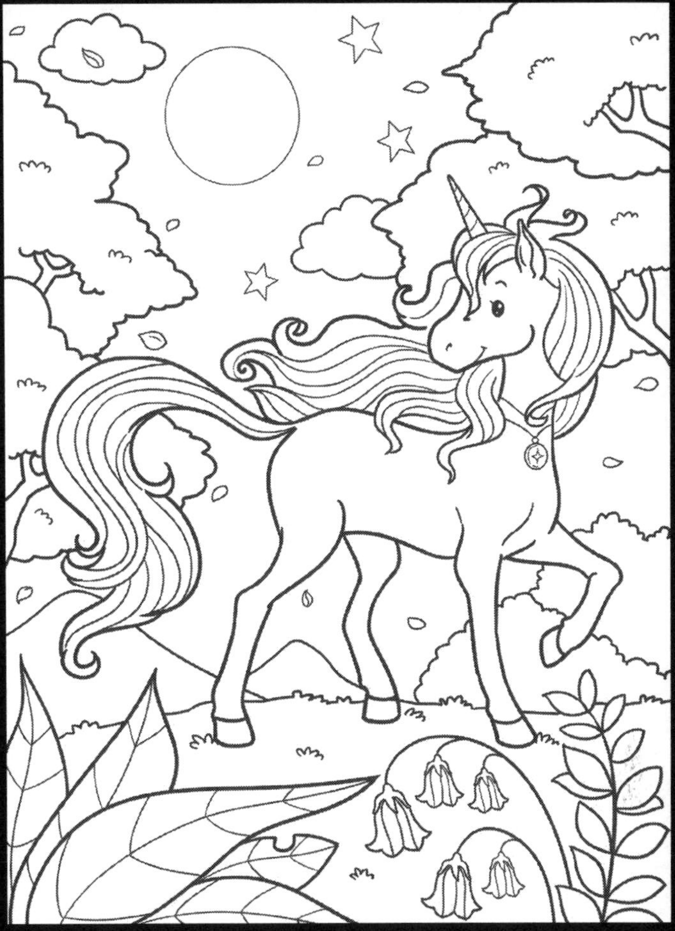

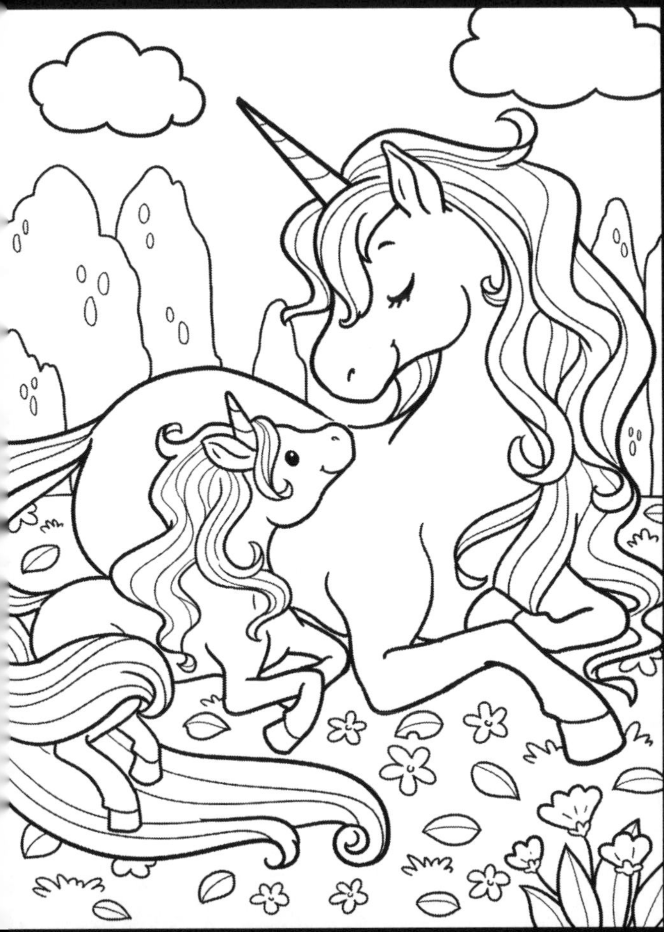

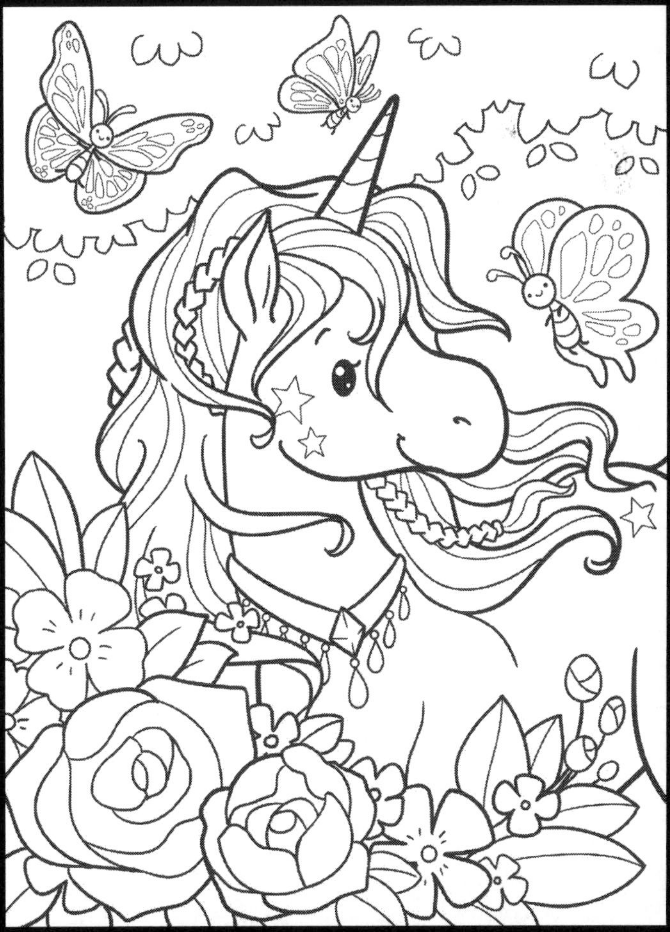

COLOR TESTING

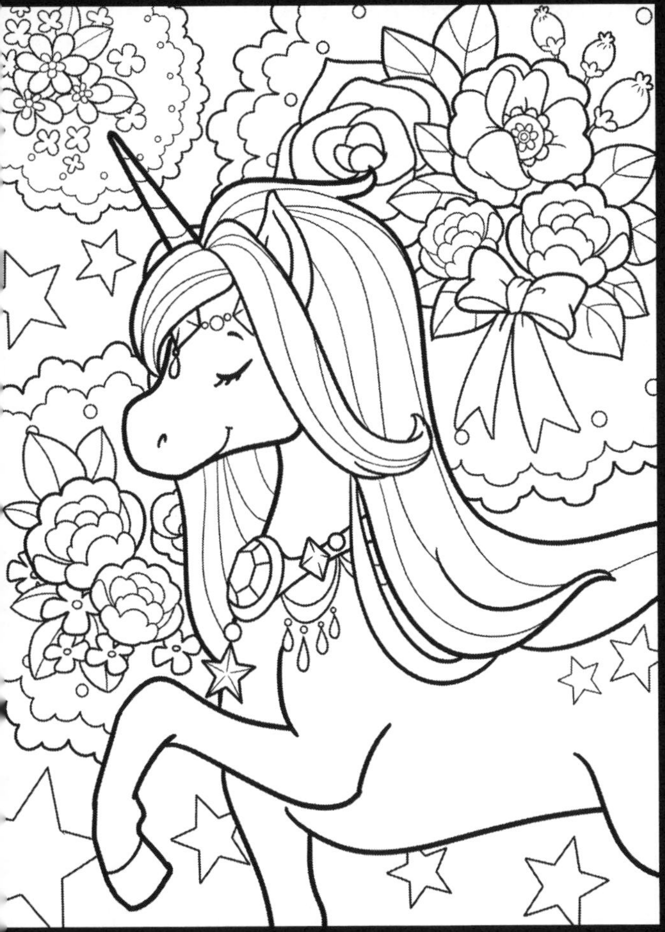

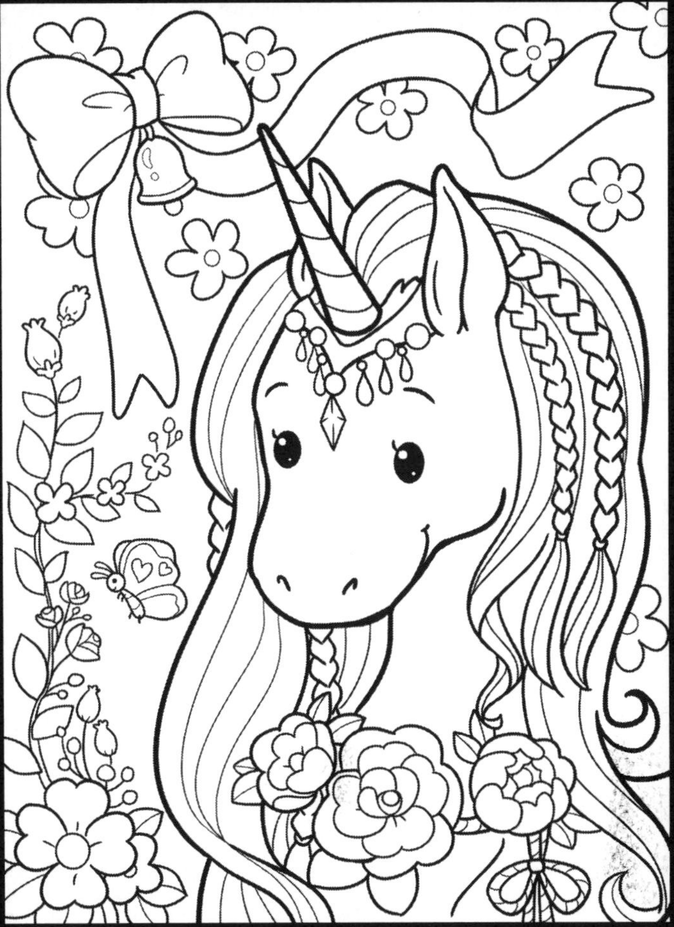

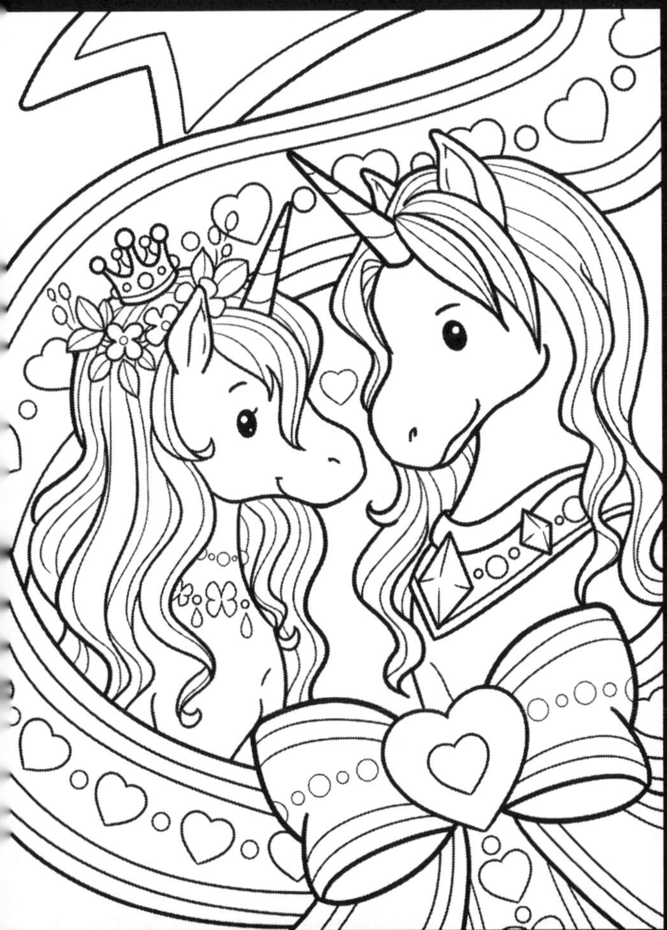

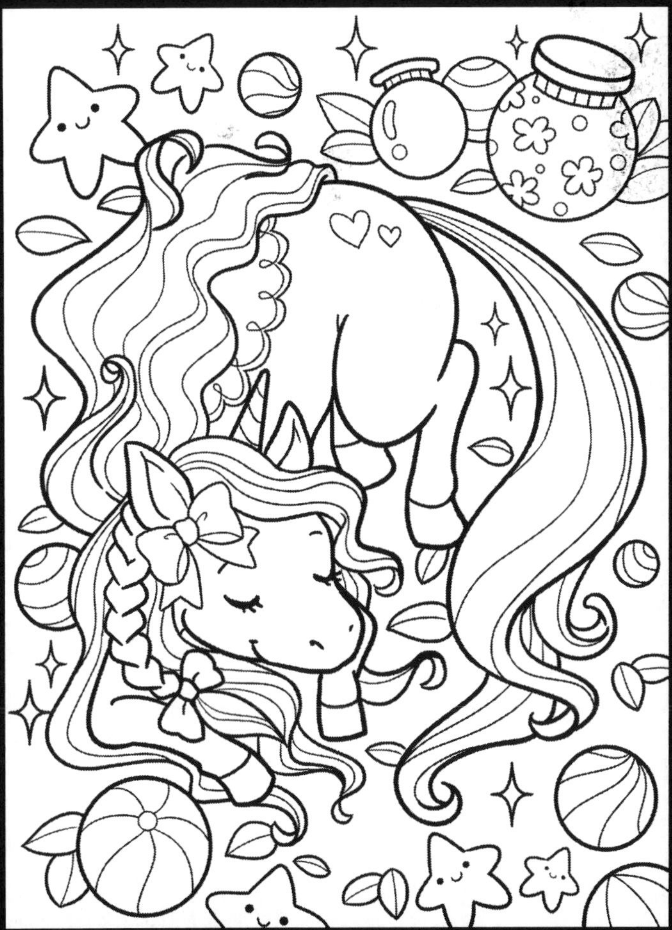

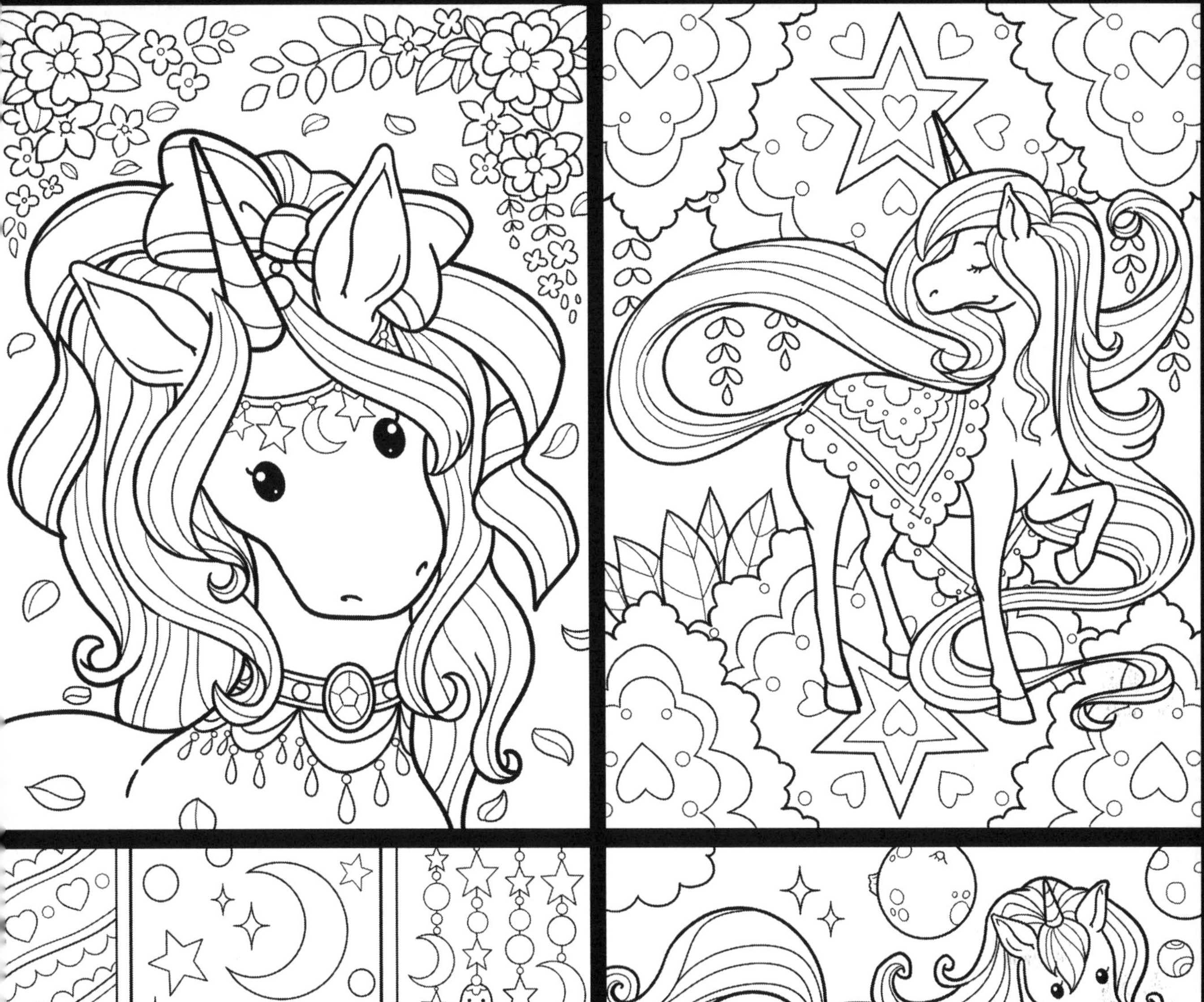
Z
Z
Z

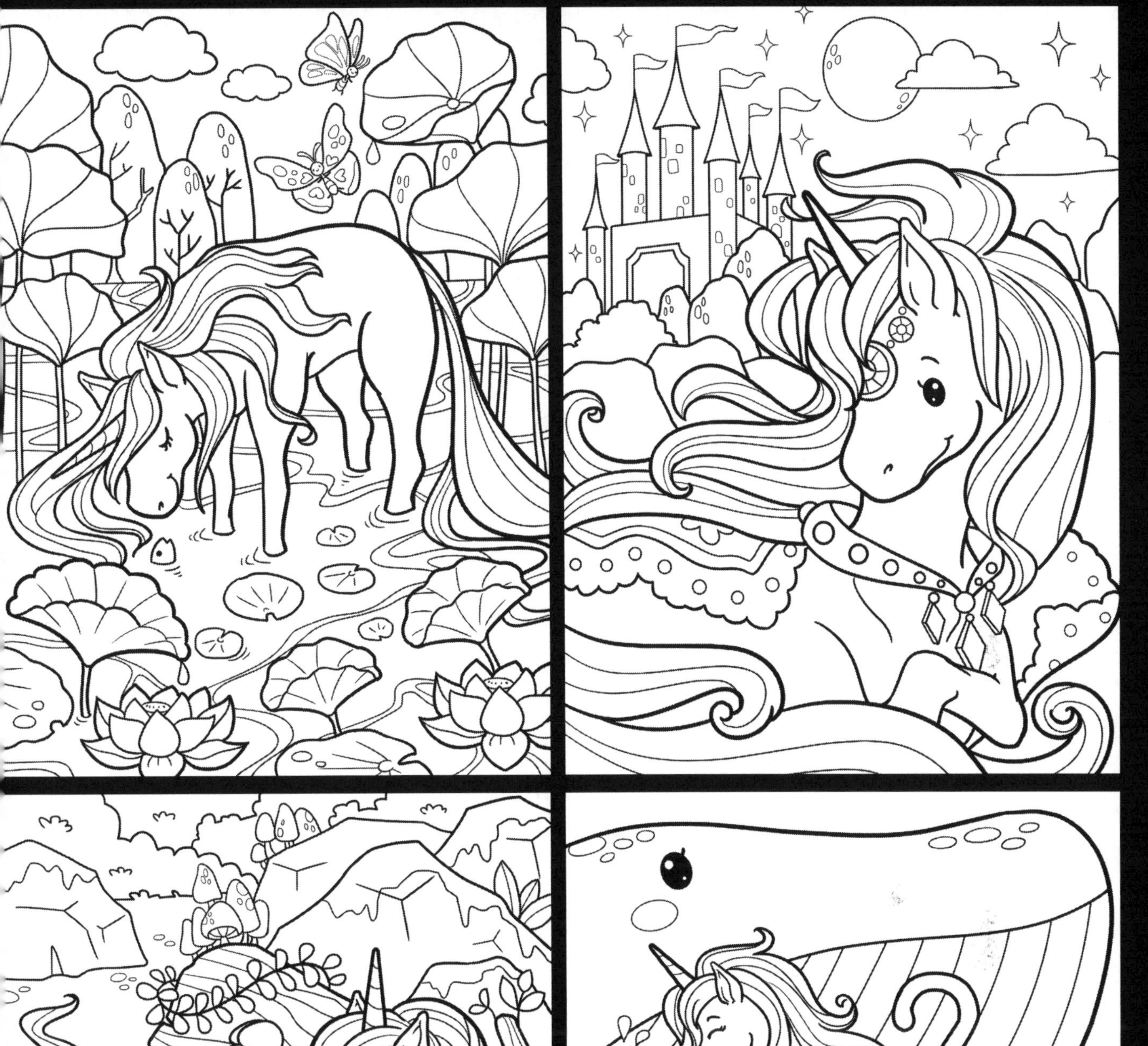

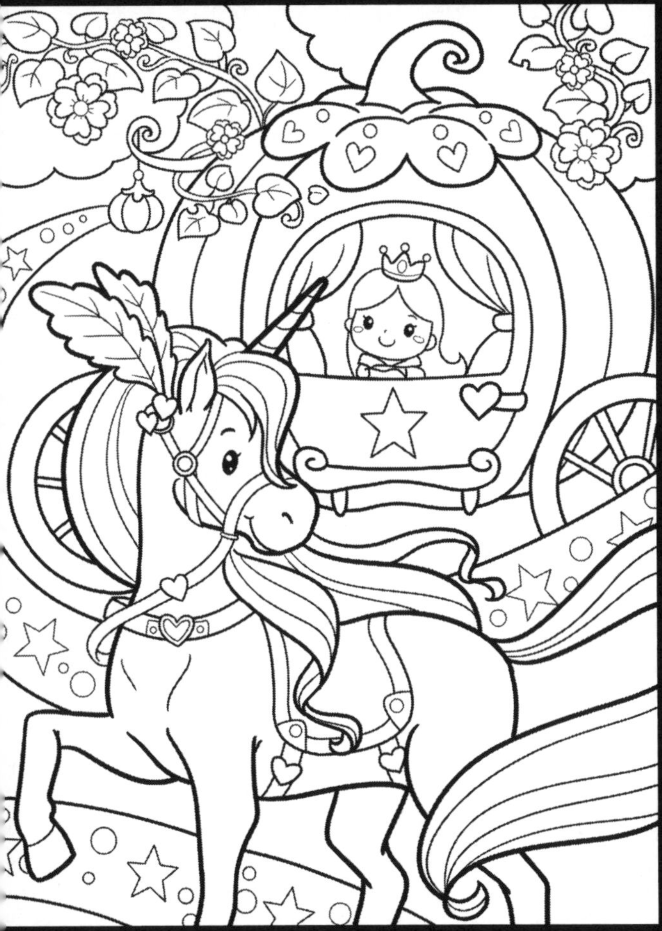

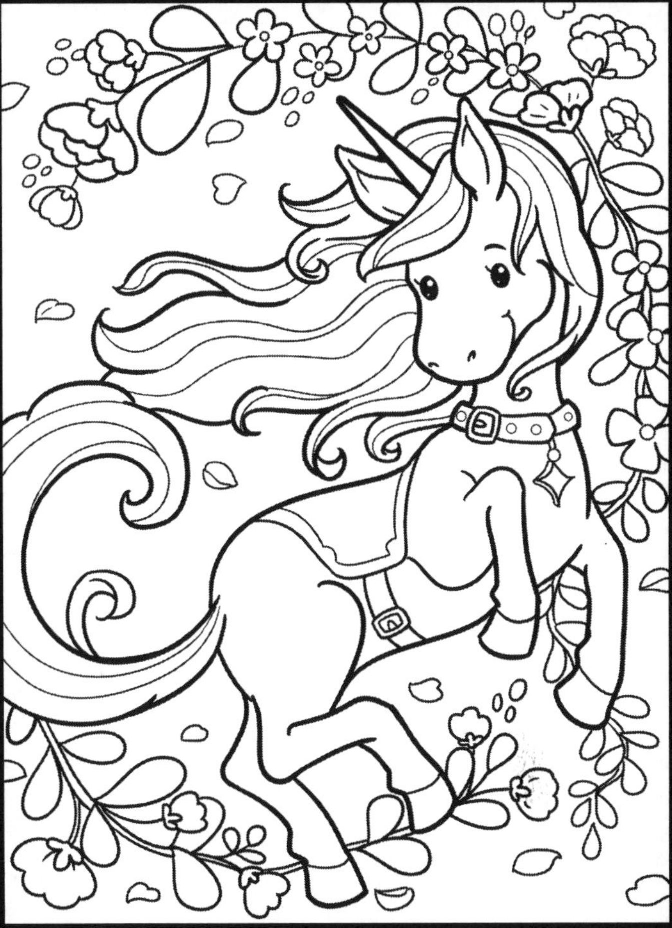

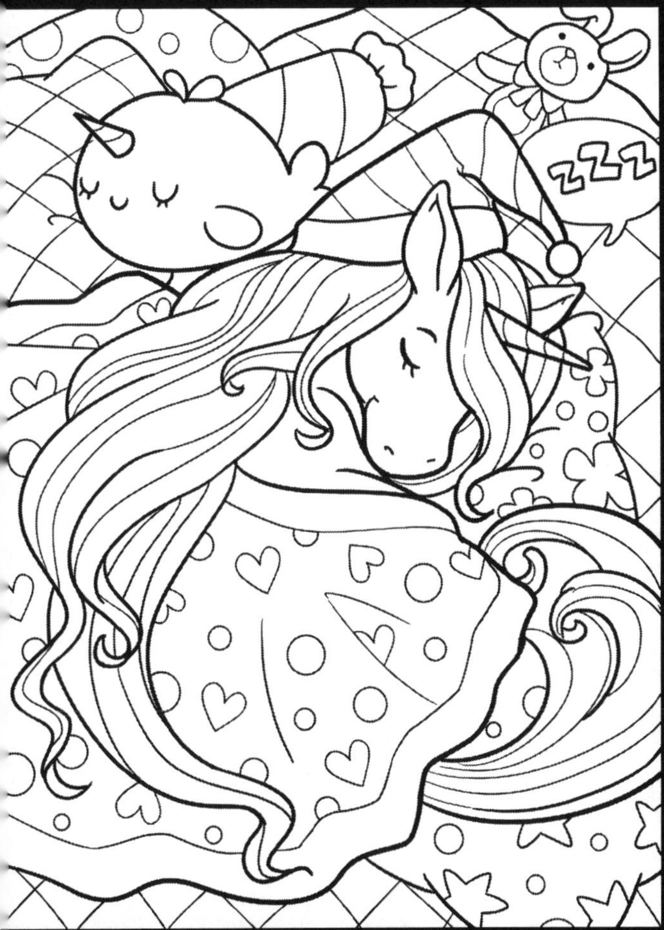
ZZZ

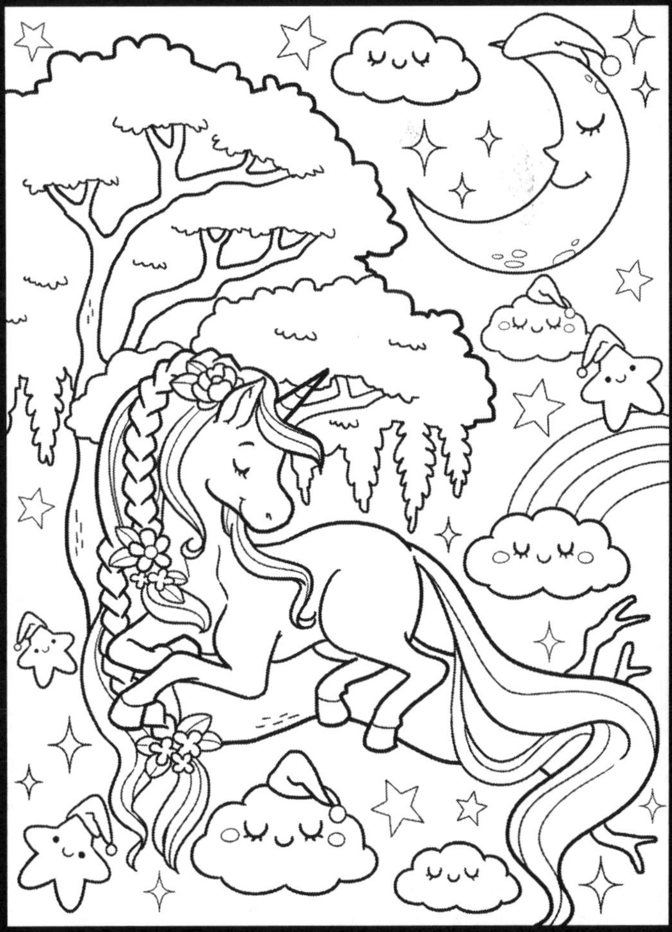

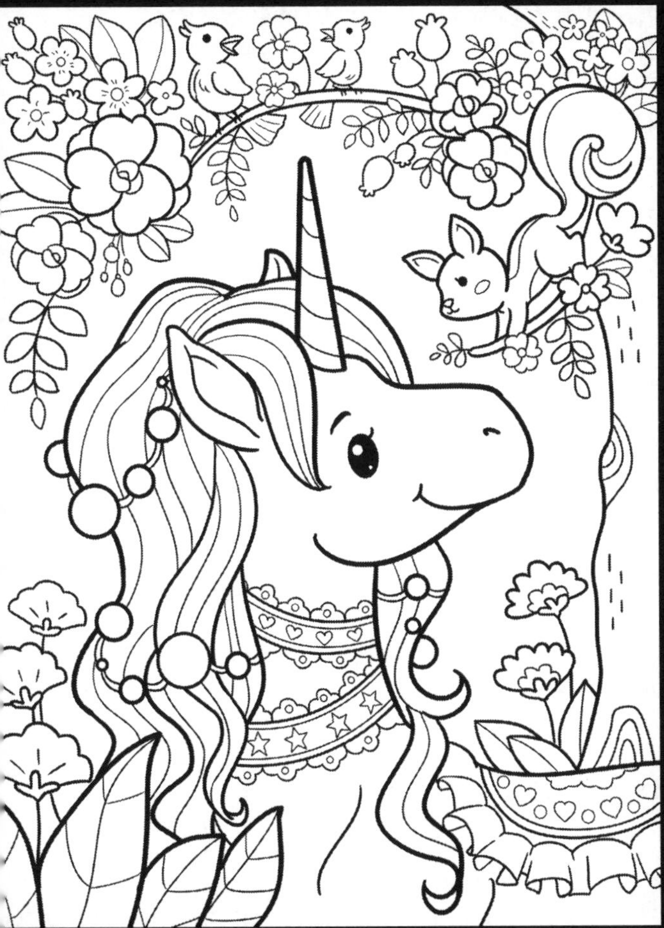

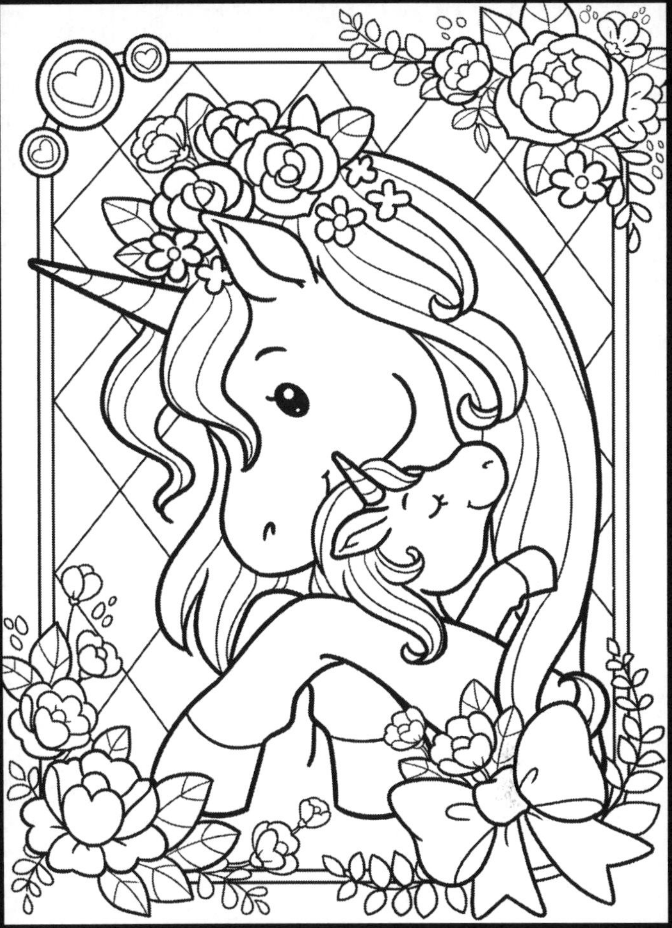

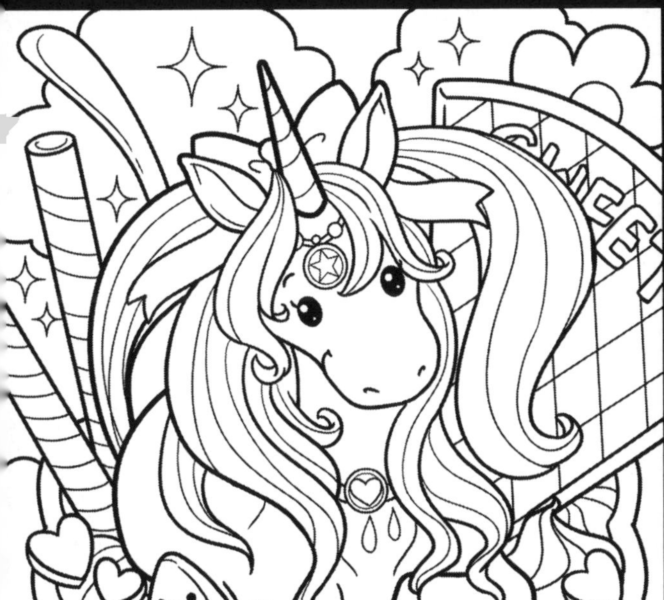

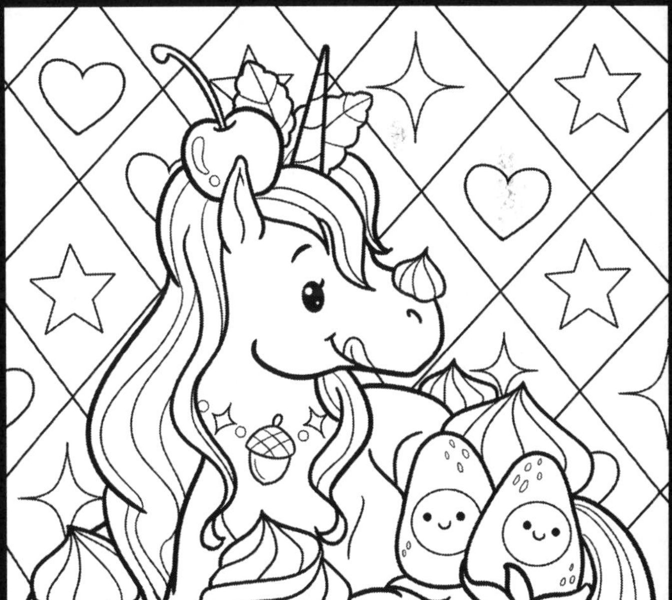

Yesss! you did it!
Thanks for choosing our coloring book, Yeahhh :)

Welcome to our Daisiejoy family!
we're so excited to give you our best coloring book,
and hope you will enjoy and fall in love with this
coloring book. If you want to support us more,
please visit our website www.daisiejoy.com
or give us a review on Amazon!

Oh! and don't forget to look at the back
of this book, we have a gift for you!

Enjoy your coloring, Love you!

Daisiejoy
Coloring book for all

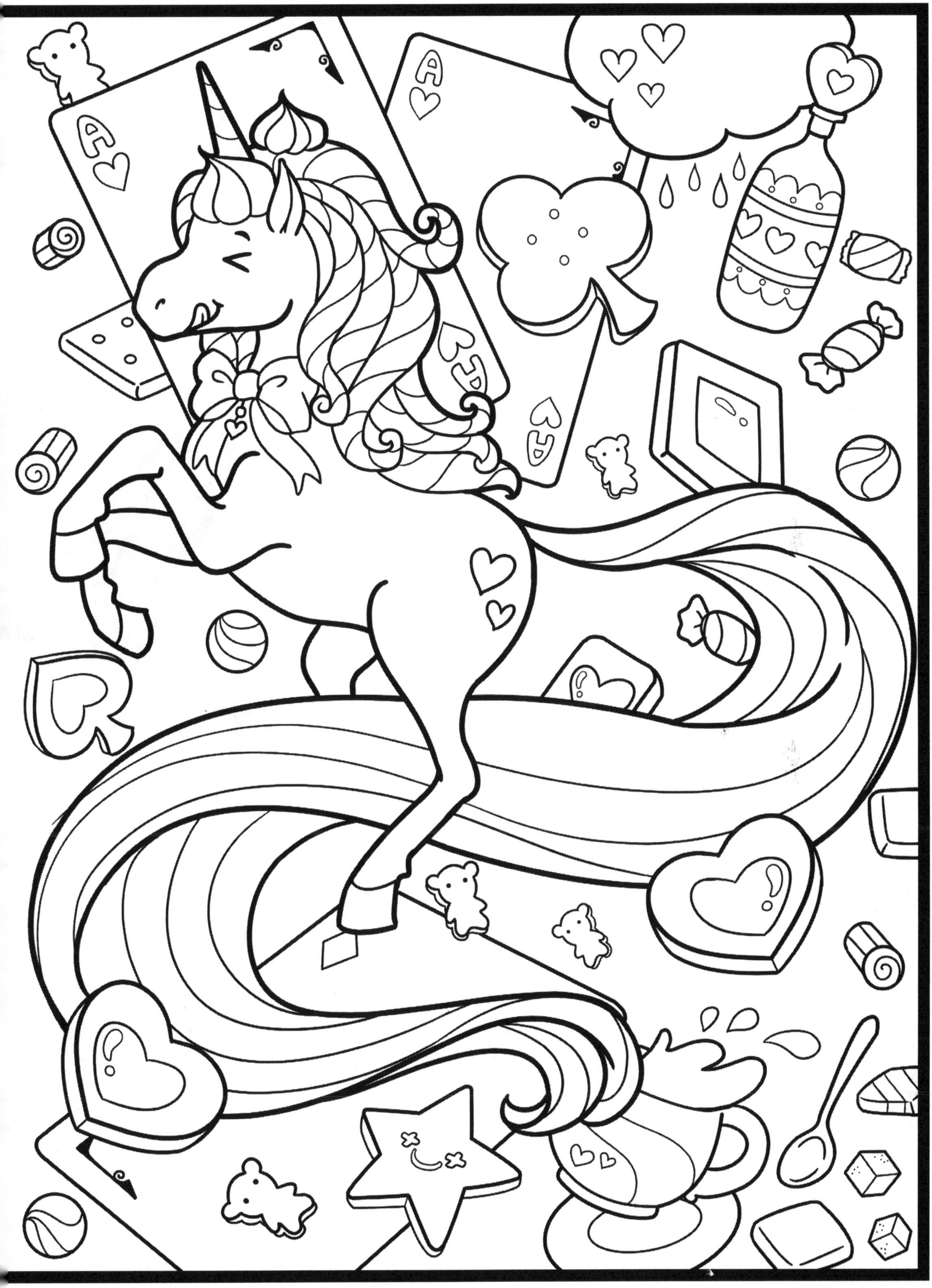

Free gifts download!
Mermaid coloring digital files

- DOWNLOAD LINK -

www.daisiejoy.com/ucus62

Leave your review

If you like this book, please leave your review
on Amazon, Your words can encourage us.
Amazon search : Daisiejoy unicorn coloring book

Review this product

Share your thoughts with other customers

Write a customer review

Our Social Media

Facebook : Daisiejoy Coloring Books
Sharing your finished artwork with the Hashtag #daisiejoy
#daisiejoycoloringbooks

Youtube : Daisiejoy Coloring Books
Subscribe our channel to stay tuned on coloring VDO

Instagram : @daisiejoy
Sharing your finished artwork with the Hashtag #daisiejoy
#daisiejoycoloringbooks

Our Shop

Please visit our online shop.

Daisiejoy.com

Amazon.com

Check out our other coloring books!
search Daisiejoy on Amazon.com

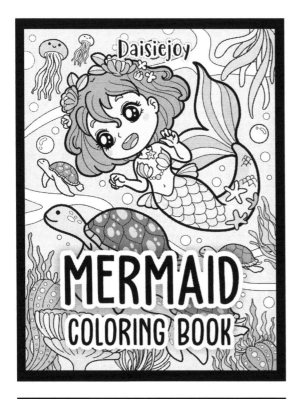

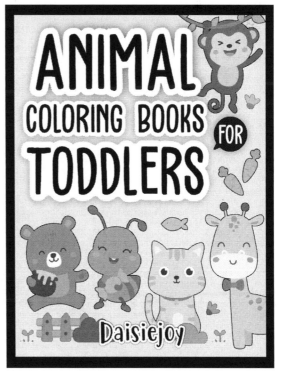

Check out our other activity books for kids!
search Daisiejoy Activity on Amazon.com

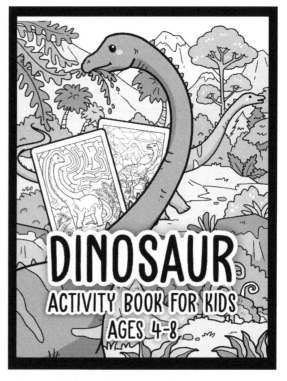

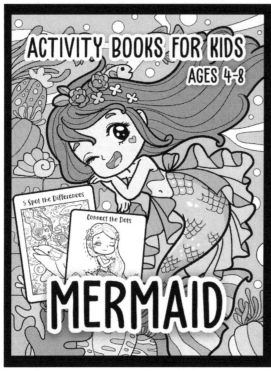

Daisiejoy

MERMAID
COLORING BOOK

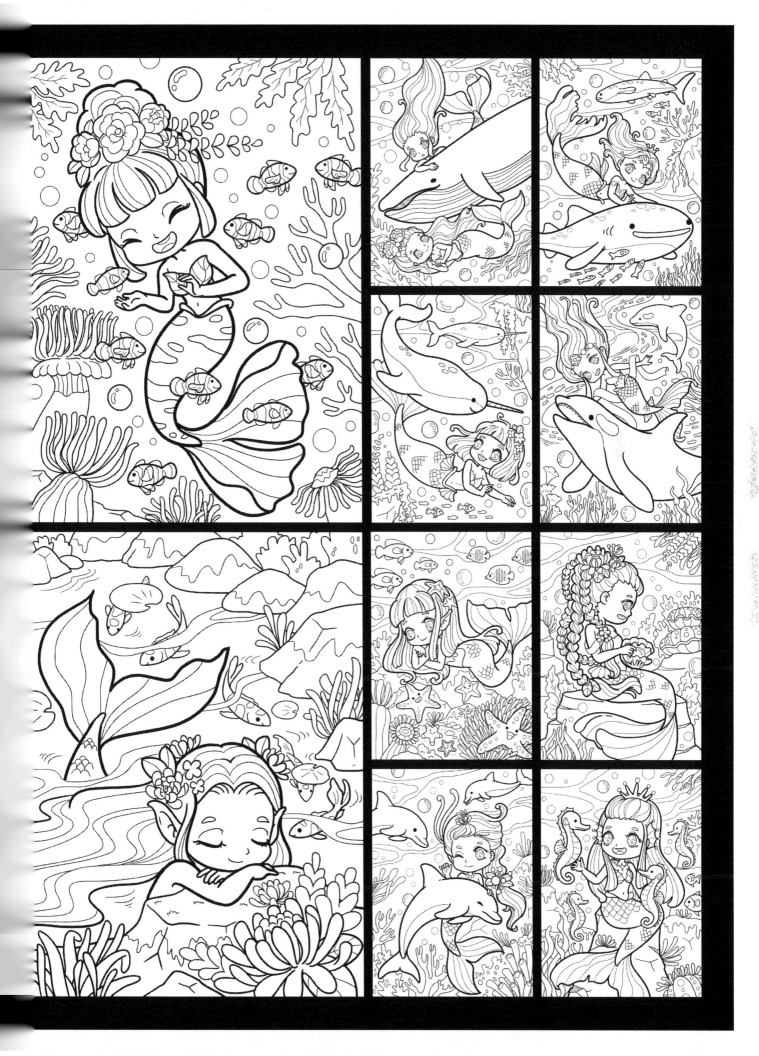

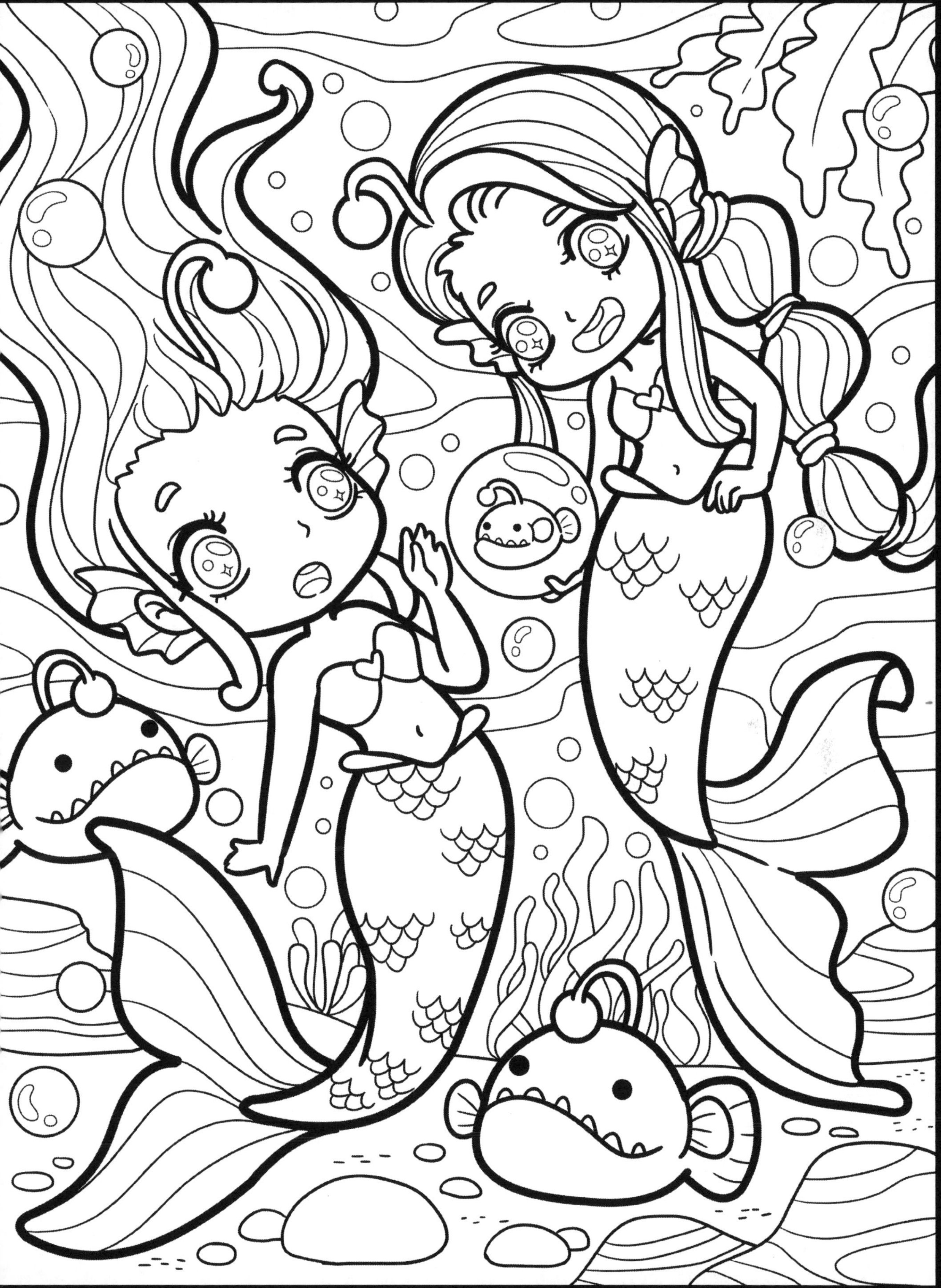

Daisiejoy

DINOSAUR COLORING BOOK

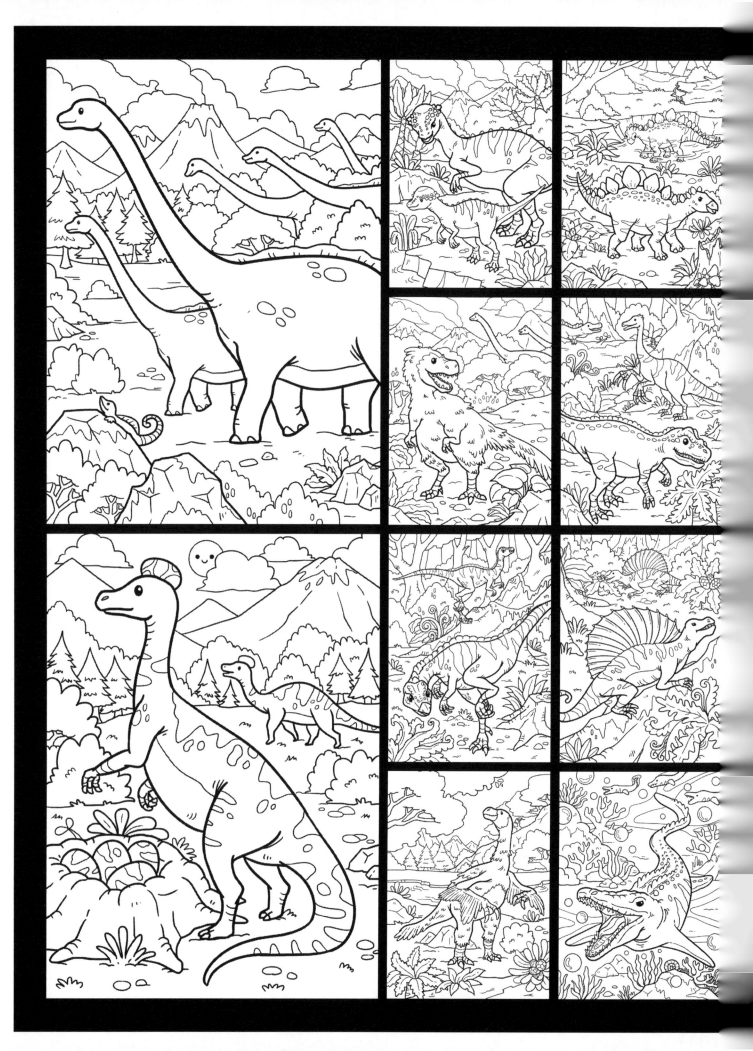

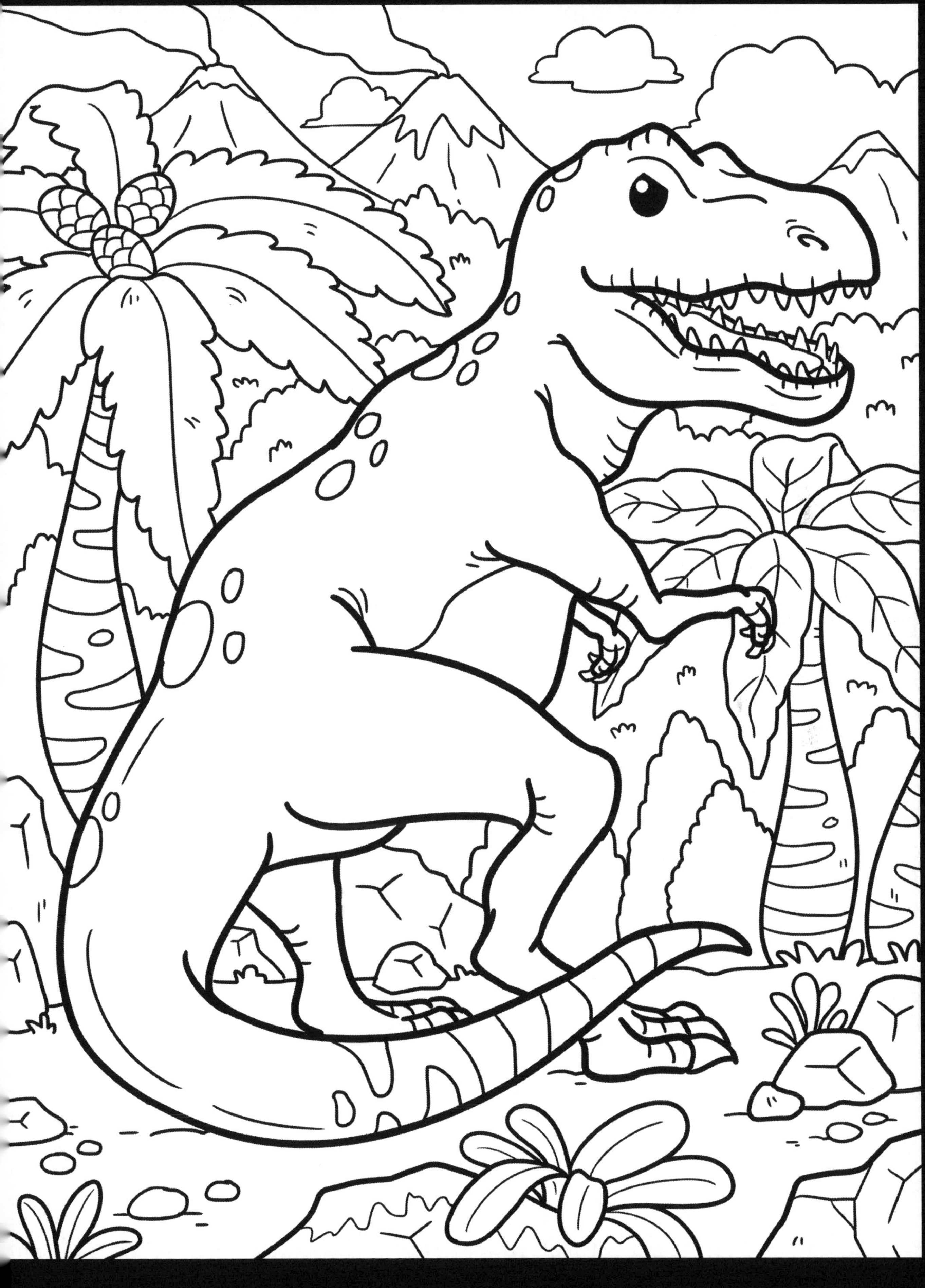